# LIFE IN
# Ancient
# Egypt

Written by
**William Crouch**

Illustrated by
**Robin Lawrie**

**Derrydale Books**
New York

**A TEMPLAR BOOK**

This 1990 edition published by
Derrydale Books
distributed by Crown Publishers, Inc.,
225 Park Avenue South, New York, New York 10003

Devised and produced by The Templar Company plc
Pippbrook Mill, London Road, Dorking, Surrey RH4 1JE, Great Britain

**Editor** Andy Charman
**Designer** Jane Hunt

Printed and bound in Italy

ISBN 0-517-03554-5

h g f e d c b a

# Contents

# The Nile

My name is Kha and I am eight years old. I live in Thebes, and I go to school in the temple at Karnak.

At school our teacher, Anpu, told us about the wonders of the Nile.

"It was given to us by the god, Hapi," he said. "It is the world's longest river and without it Egypt would be desert. Many thousands of years ago, our land was cooler. There was much rain and rich soil. Elephants, lions, giraffes, and buffalo lived in the dense forests and the people were great hunters.

"Then, gradually, the land became hotter, there was less rainfall and the trees and grass began to die. The animals moved into the African jungle.

"Hapi sent water from Africa by the White Nile but this was not enough. So every year he sends torrents of water down the Blue Nile from the great mountains in the east. The two rivers join giving water for our cattle and rich, black soil for our crops.

"There are times when we have too much water. Houses are flooded and animals drowned. Or we have too little and the crops die."

On the way home, my friend, Sedi, and I walked along the banks of the Nile. We watched people making bricks and cooking-pots with mud. Nearby, men were cutting papyrus, which grow as reeds on the marshy banks. On the river itself, men were fishing from papyrus boats.

"Without the Nile," said Sedi, "there would be no Egypt."

At home that evening everyone was excited. The next day, the Pharaoh, Ramesses II, was returning to his palace after the war with the Hittites. There was to be a grand procession.

Kha    Sedi

6

Bricks and pots are made with the thick, black mud from the river. They are left to bake in the sun.

Papyrus is harvested to make paper for the Royal Palace. Bundles of it are used to make small boats.

The Nile is teeming with fish. The men catch them from their papyrus boats.

# Great Pharaohs

Early the next morning, Sedi and I made our way to the center of the city. The city had been decorated with bunches of palm leaves. Already, there were hundreds of people waiting.

Everyone cheered when the soldiers appeared with their brightly painted chariots. Then they roared with delight when the Pharaoh came riding by with his captain and chief armor bearer. He looked very grand.

"He is a great hero!" cried Sedi. "My father says he charged alone against 2,500 chariots of the enemy."

"We have had many great kings," I said. "Remember Egypt's first ruler, King Menes, who defeated the Hamitic tribes and set up the kingdoms of Upper and Lower Egypt."

"Yes," Sedi agreed, "and King Zoser with his vizier, Imhotep, who built the first pyramid."

The Pharaohs are loved and respected by everyone. They have the spirit of the falcon god Horus, who is master of the sky.

"We mustn't forget Tuthmosis III," I said. "He was a soldier, explorer, and conqueror of many lands. He also hunted elephants in the dreaded swamps of Niy and he built the fine temples at Karnak."

At last the procession ended. The Pharaoh entered his palace and we went home to my father's farm.

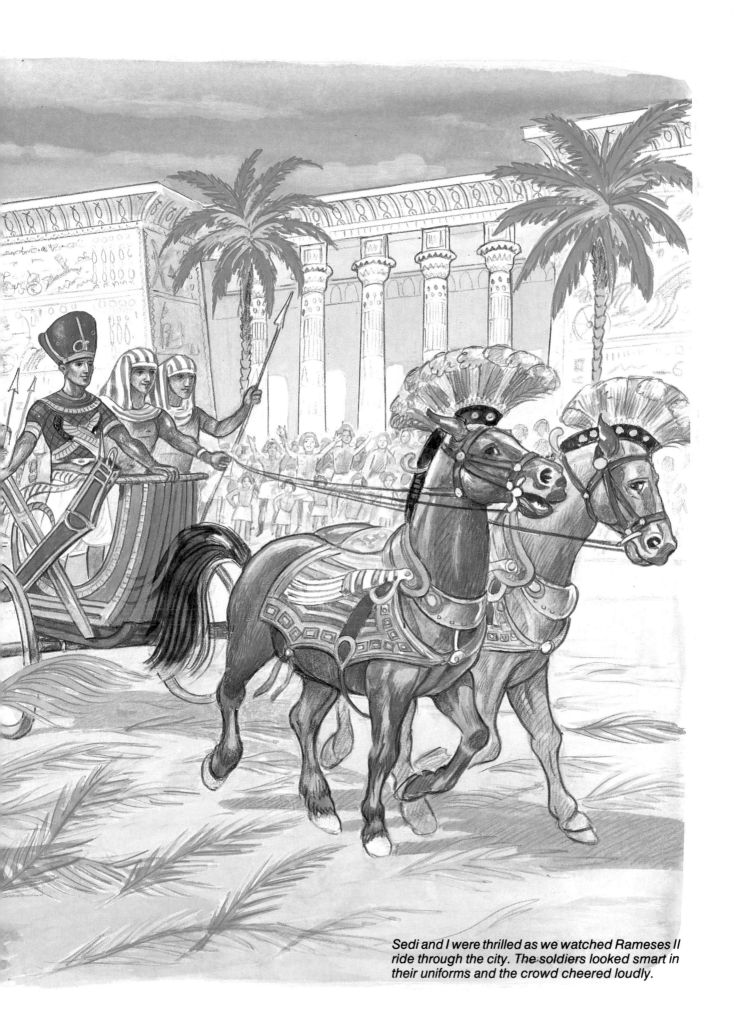

Sedi and I were thrilled as we watched Rameses II ride through the city. The soldiers looked smart in their uniforms and the crowd cheered loudly.

# On the farm

Sedi stayed with my family that evening.

"Everyone must help with the harvest," said my father. "This year the Nile god has been kind to us."

Each year I help to dig the channels which take water from the Nile to the fields. Every evening when I come home from school I use the shaduf to water the crops.

Very early the next morning everyone started work. I loaded Ben, my donkey, with the corn my father had cut and took it to the threshing floor. When it had been trampled, Sedi raked the grain into heaps.

My mother and Taheb, my sister, and our women servants winnowed the grain. First, they scooped the grain into winnowing baskets. Then they tossed it into the air and the wind took the chaff away. Ben then carried the grain to our granary where it will be stored ready for making bread and beer.

In the afternoon Sedi and I went into the garden.

"This is where we grow our fruit and vegetables," I told him. "Come to the back of the house and see the goats and the sheep."

"You are always busy," said Sedi.

"Yes, next year we plan to grow some flax for making linen."

"Back to work, Kha," called my father. "When the harvest is finished I have a surprise for you both."

Keeping the flood water on the fields is hard work. In the past, farmers dug ditches around their fields and filled them with water from the river. Leather buckets were used to keep the ditches full.

These days, we keep the ditches full using a shaduf. This is a long pole with a bucket on one end and a stone on the other. We lower the bucket into the river and the counterbalancing weight makes it easier to lift out again. Then we swing the pole around and empty the bucket into the ditch.

After the floods we break up the soil and then dig deep furrows with plows pulled by oxen. We sow the seeds and then drive sheep or goats across the fields to trample them down. When we have harvested the crop, we spread it out on to firm ground and make the oxen walk on it. This breaks off the husks. Then it is winnowed.

11

# Egypt's lawmakers

The next morning Harkuf, a scribe, came to the farm.

"It is time to pay the tax," he said.

My father scowled. He was not pleased to see Harkuf.

"I know exactly how much you owe," Harkuf said.

Harkuf called his servants and they took away several baskets of grain. These would go to the royal granary as tax payments.

*Scribes visit a farm to work out how much tax the farmer should pay. They count the cattle and measure the fields.*

"What would happen if a farmer did not pay?" I asked.

"We have strict punishments for people who refuse to pay," said the scribe. "In Egypt, the Pharaoh owns everything. He commands the army and makes the laws. He has a chief minister called a vizier. Most government officials come from noble families and may be relatives of the Pharaoh. The country is divided into provinces called nomes and each one is governed by an official called a nomarch."

"Will you always be a tax collector?" Sedi asked.

"No," Harkuf said. "I may see that the Pharaoh's laws are kept. I could become a nomarch and rule a province or I might even rise to be the vizier of all Egypt.

"Scribes are very important people. Without them Egypt could not be governed. We are able to accomplish this because we have been educated."

*Law breakers are beaten or thrown into the Nile to be eaten by crocodiles. They could be sent to work in the palace or even have their ears cut off.*

*One of the scribes' most important tasks is to equip the army for one of the Pharaoh's expeditions. Here, a scribe sends out food and weapons.*

# Language and writing

"I have been to school since I was four," I said excitedly, "and now I am eight. Can I be a scribe?"

"Yes, Kha," Harkuf answered, "but you must attend school until you are 16 and work very hard. A scribe must read well and do neat writing."

"Picture writing is difficult," I said.

"Hieroglyphs are not easy," said Harkuf. "You know that a hieroglyphic picture may mean a whole word, or an idea, or it may mean just a sound."

"Yes," I replied "a drawing of a house is the word for house but a loaf of bread gives the sound 't'."

*If I am going to be a scribe, I will have to understand the hieroglyphs so that I can read the sacred messages in the tombs and temples. Sedi and I practice writing hieroglyphs for hours every day on wooden tablets or pieces of pottery. There are more than 700 signs.*

"Well done," Harkuf said, smiling. "Later you will use the hieratic writing which is easier and faster. And you will write on papyrus."

As Harkuf prepared to leave, he turned to me and called.

"Don't forget you will have to learn mathematics and astronomy, as well as letter writing, before you can become a scribe."

I waved goodbye to Harkuf and turned to Sedi.

"I want to be a scribe, don't you?"

"Perhaps," said Sedi, "but I think I would rather be a priest."

To make paper from papyrus, the reeds, which are harvested from the banks of the Nile, are first cut into strips.

A horizontal layer of strips is placed over a vertical layer forming a sheet.

The sheet is beaten with a wooden mallet. The juice sticks the strips together.

The sheet is rolled with a round stone to make it flat and smooth and ready for use.

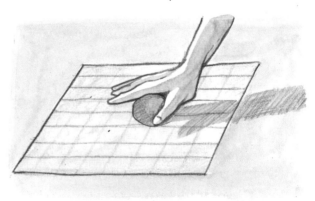

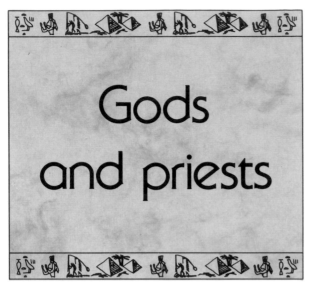

# Gods and priests

We worked hard gathering the harvest. After two weeks my father told us it was time we had a holiday.

"Let's go to the temple," Sedi suggested.

Hori, the priest, met us at the huge gateway.

"There is no school today," he reminded us.

"Sedi would like to be a priest," I said. "Can you tell him about your work?"

"Of course, and I will explain how we serve the gods."

He invited us into the courtyard.

"This is the greatest temple ever built," he said. "It is the home of Amun, the god of Thebes and the king of all gods. At the back of the temple there is a sanctuary where only priests can go.

"Each day the High Priest enters the sanctuary and opens the shrine where the god is resting. The priest will bathe and dress Amun in fresh garments. Then he will offer him food."

"We have a god at home," said Sedi. "His name is Bes."

"Most houses have their own gods," said Hori. "They bring good luck and happiness to the family."

He smiled and turned to leave us.

"I must go now," he said. "Tomorrow I am going to visit the pyramids on the other side of the Nile. Be here early and you can come too."

*There are many gods in Egypt: Re is the sun god and Anubis is the god of life and death. Amun is the lord of the throwns and the god of Karnak. Bes is a household god, we have a statue of Bes on our farm.*

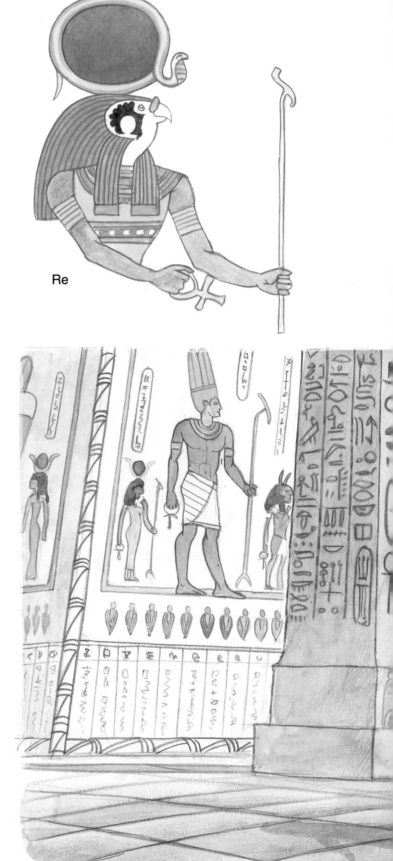

Re

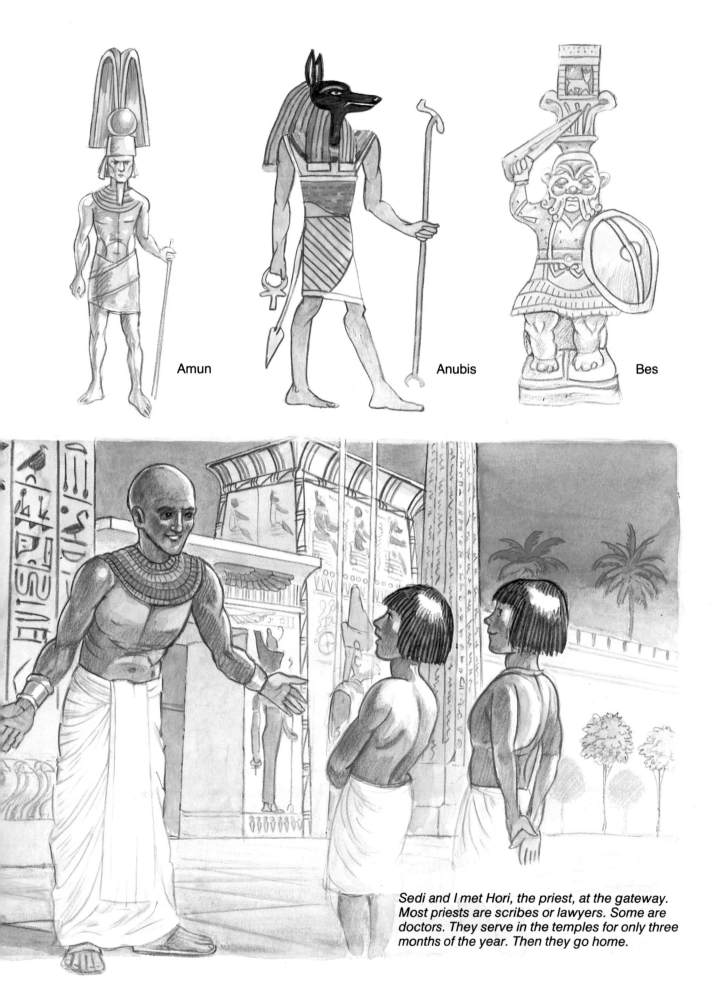

Amun

Anubis

Bes

Sedi and I met Hori, the priest, at the gateway. Most priests are scribes or lawyers. Some are doctors. They serve in the temples for only three months of the year. Then they go home.

17

# Pyramids

The pyramid was built more than two hundred years ago. Giant ramps of sand and rubble were made and thousands of men using palm-fiber ropes hauled the blocks into place.

We met Hori early the next morning and crossed the Nile in a papyrus boat. For most of the journey Sedi talked to Hori about being a priest.

Eventually, we arrived in the desert and there was the huge pyramid.

"It is really a vast tomb," said Hori, "built to give the Pharaoh all he would need for a wonderful afterlife.

"The stone was dug from quarries farther down the Nile. Square blocks were cut and floated on rafts to the building site. Inside the pyramid is the burial chamber. Here the Pharaoh will have furniture, clothes, jewelry, and models of his servants.

"This pyramid was built more than two hundred years ago," continued Hori. "Since the time of Tuthmosis I the Pharaohs have been buried in tombs dug deeply into the cliffs."

At that moment a boy came running towards them.

"It is Aktoy," said the priest. "He is the son of a nobleman."

"I have just been to visit my grandfather's tomb," cried Aktoy. "It has been entered by robbers. I must tell my father."

"I must attend a nobleman's funeral today," said Hori. "Anpu has agreed that you should come with me."

We crossed the Nile and waited for the funeral procession to arrive.

"The body has been prepared for the afterlife," said Hori. "It will have a painted mask and be placed in a decorated coffin."

We watched as the funeral barge arrived at the landing stage. The procession began its journey up the rocky path to the tomb.

At the tombside, Hori helped other priests to carry out the ceremonies. They chanted magic spells while

Before a funeral, skilled people called embalmers mummify the body by anointing it with oils and ointments. Then they wrap it in linen bandages. Doctors have learned a lot about medicines and bodies by assisting the embalmers.

The coffin was on a sledge built like a boat and pulled by four oxen. Women mourners followed, tearing at their clothes, throwing sand over their heads, and wailing. It was an eerie sound.

The nobleman's tomb had been beautifully painted with his favorite pictures. Many people had worked to make him comfortable. Sculptors, jewelers, and coffin makers all helped.

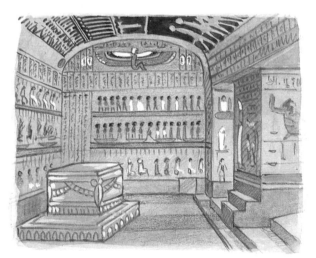

dancers chased evil spirits away.

"He will be very happy in the afterlife," Hori said later.

At the landing stage we met Aktoy.

"Good news," he said. "A scribe had drawn pictures of the stolen jewelry before it was placed in my grandfather's tomb. Come to my house and see them. Perhaps you can help me catch the robbers."

19

# Egyptian houses

*A nobleman's house has a walled vineyard and a leisure garden with a small lake. Storehouses, stables, a well, and animal pens are near the servants' quarters. In a corner of the outer courtyard is a large granary.*

Hori returned to the temple and we went with Aktoy to see the pictures.

His house was surrounded by a high wall. At the main entrance the gatekeeper welcomed us. A path lined with trees led to the family temple but Aktoy took us through a smaller gateway and into the main courtyard.

"Come into the house," he said.

We climbed steps to a porch and went into a large, beautifully decorated room. There were columns of richly plastered wood supporting a brightly colored ceiling. The walls were high and painted in soft colors with pictures of flowers and birds. There were small barred windows near the ceiling. These let in light and air but kept the room cool and shady.

"This is the central hall," said Aktoy.

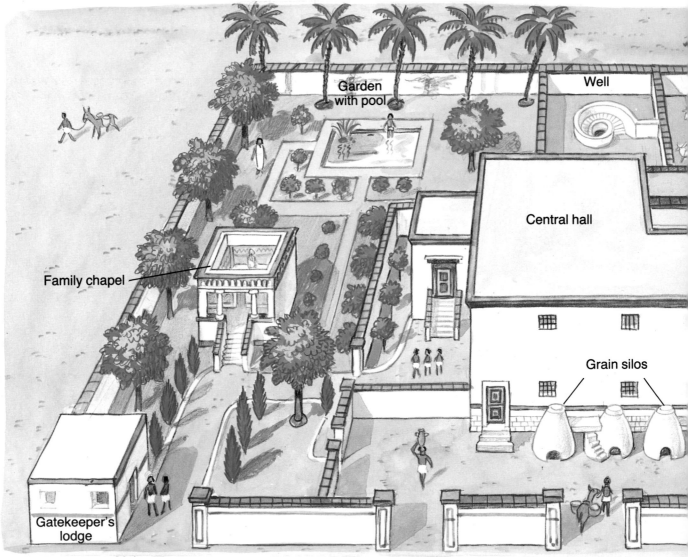

Garden with pool

Well

Central hall

Family chapel

Grain silos

Gatekeeper's lodge

Main entrance

"There are guestrooms, bathrooms, a kitchen, and private rooms for my parents. Shall we go upstairs?"

From the roof we could see the buildings and gardens around the house.

"What an amazing place this is!" said Sedi.

"What sort of house do you live in?" asked Aktoy.

"A farm," I said. "A main hall, an outer room for greeting strangers on one side of it and bedrooms on the other. We cook and wash outside."

"I live in the city," said Sedi. "We have a similar house to Kha's but with no garden."

"Some people have only a single, mud-brick room, which they have to share with their animals," I reminded him.

*We followed Aktoy into the central hall of his house. Sedi and I gazed in wonder as Aktoy pointed out the richly colored ceiling and the huge, decorated columns.*

*After the harvest, servants carry grain to the silos. Here it is stored. Later it will be used to make bread and beer.*

Cattle pens

Store rooms and servants' quarters

Kitchens

Stables

Chariot house

# Craftsmen

"Here are the pictures of the stolen jewelry," said Aktoy. "See the sign of a snake on each one?"

"My father may be able to help," suggested Sedi. "He is a furniture maker and has worked with jewelers at the Pharaoh's palace. Shall we go and ask him?"

On the way to his house, Sedi talked about Pemerah, his father.

"He has worked at the palace for King Ramesses II," he said, "and for the High Priest in the temple at Karnak. He has also made some beautiful furniture for the royal tomb.

*There are goldsmiths, artists, and sculptors as well as carpenters and builders working for the*

*Pharaoh. They are paid with bread but sometimes they are given gifts of wine or meat.*

"At the moment he is working at home making things that he can sell in the local market."

"We have many craftsmen on our estate," said Aktoy. "They make everything you can think of from bronze statues to shoes."

When we got to Sedi's house Pemerah told us what to do.

"There is a man selling jewelry in the market," he said. "He is not honest and he may have the stolen articles."

We ran to the market and soon found the stall. There were displays of brightly colored garments, kilts of pleated linen, and leather belts with silver buckles.

At the back of the stall, partly hidden by some colored necklaces, were bracelets and brooches with the sign of the snake.

"Keep watch!" said Aktoy excitedly. "I will get my father. He will bring a scribe to question the man and servants to arrest him."

*There were many stalls in the market and lots of people all around. The stall was not difficult to find. Atkoy knew he must act quickly before the stolen jewelry was sold. Sedi and I kept watch while Aktoy rushed off to find his father.*

23

# Egypt at play

Noblemen hunt lions in the grasslands to the south or crocodiles and hippopotami on the river banks.

Aktoy's father, Baalry, was pleased.

"I must give you a reward," he said. "Tomorrow I am going to take Aktoy on a hunting trip. You can come, too. Have you any brothers?"

"No, but I have a small sister," I said.

"Girls can't go hunting," said Baalry, "but she can spend the day playing games with my daughters."

We crossed the Nile early the next morning and drove to the sand hills to hunt hyenas and gazelles. I had never ridden in a chariot before. I found it difficult at first to keep my balance. In my chariot was an archer as well as a charioteer. We shot a lot of animals.

"I enjoy hunting," said Baalry, "particularly chasing lions in the grasslands farther south, or crocodiles and hippopotami on the river banks."

"My father has hunted waterfowl with boomerangs," I said, "and he enjoys fishing with a spear. My mother prefers to go to the religious festivals and likes to watch wrestling."

Later we returned to Aktoy's house and Taheb ran to meet me.

"I've had a lovely day," she said. "Aktoy's sisters have a board game called senet. It's more interesting than playing with my dolls."

Later we joined the family for a wonderful meal in the central hall.

"I shall not forget today," Sedi remarked as we said goodbye.

Taheb enjoyed herself playing with Aktoy's sisters in the leisure garden. They played leap frog and ball catching and learned a new dance in honor of Hathor, the goddess of joy.

The board game that Taheb played with Aktoy's sisters is great fun. It is a game of skill and chance. Taheb quickly learned the rules and was delighted when she beat Aktoy's sisters.

# Travel and trade

A week passed. Then, one morning my father woke me very early.

"The harvest is finished, Kha," he said, "and now for the surprise I promised you."

We were going up the Nile to Nubia where we would barter our goods for cattle. We loaded grain and papyrus on to a sailing boat.

"This is the largest boat I have been on," said Sedi.

The sailors had just returned from the port of Byblos. They had come to Thebes with cedar wood, copper, silver, and precious stones.

"Our greatest expedition was to the Land of Punt," said one of them. "We took beads, trinkets, and papyrus scrolls and brought back ivory, ebony, and living myrrh trees."

"We have to collect some gold," another sailor explained. "Most of the Pharaoh's treasures are paid for with gold taken from Nubia."

At Abu Simbel our boat passed by the temple that Ramesses II was building. Then we came to a trading post guarded by a stone fortress. We exchanged our goods for cattle and a sailor bartered linen for ostrich

*Many of the things we need come from other countries. We have more grain than we need, and papyrus and flax to spare. We can use these goods to buy others.*

feathers and animal skins.

To decide what the goods were worth a scribe worked out their value in a fixed weight of gold.

"We call this fixed value a deben," he said. "It can be in gold, silver, or copper."

Soon, we had sold all our goods. It had been an exciting day. On the journey home, Sedi and I counted all the boats we could see on the river. There was everything from small papyrus boats to huge, sea-going ships.

As we watched the boats, I thought how one day, when I was older, I would write down all my adventures so that people could read them in the future . . .

*The Nile flows from south to north, but the wind usually blows in the opposite direction. On the journey to Nubia, we didn't need sails and the rowing was easy. On the way back, we used full sail.*

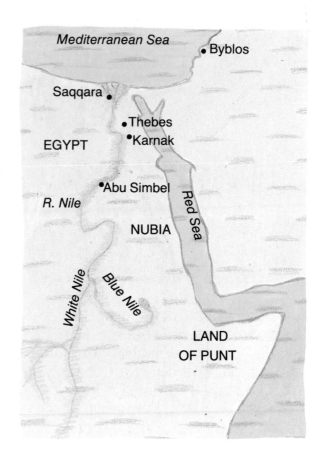

*There are a great many different kinds of boats on the Nile. There are tiny papyrus rafts, huge cargo* ships carrying grain, and fast moving galleys transporting the Pharaoh's soldiers.

# War and decline

My name is Rensi and I live on a farm near the old city of Thebes. Like most Egyptians, we are very poor because the Romans have conquered our land.

My uncle is a scribe and he has given me a valuable papyrus scroll. It was written by one of my own ancestors, the great scribe Kha. It tells of his adventures, with his friends Sedi and Aktoy, over a thousand years ago.

From the scroll, I have read all about King Menes, Tuthmosis III and, of course, Ramesses II whose statue I have seen at Abu Simbel.

My uncle told me about Ramesses III, the last great Pharaoh, who built a navy to defend our land from the Sea Peoples of the Mediterranean.

"Then," he said, "people from many countries came and destroyed our land. First, the Libyans attacked and ruled the land at the mouth of the Nile. The Nubians marched from the south and conquered Thebes.

"Later, the Assyrians entered Egypt, and took away our sacred treasures. The Babylonians came and then the Persians for we were too weak to protect ourselves.

"Alexander the Great from Macedonia drove out the Persians and became our Pharaoh.

"Now we are just a part of the Roman Empire. We have lost our land and our way of life. Our gods still care for us but I am afraid that one day they, too, will be taken from us."

I wondered what Kha would have thought of these events. Such a lot has changed since his time.

I have a scroll written by Kha. He lived 1,300 years ago. He has described the great Pharaohs and how they led their armies into battle.

In A.D.383, the Roman Emperor ordered the destruction of the Egyptian gods. This was just as Rensi's uncle had forseen.

The Egyptians fought hard to defend their land, but the invaders were too strong. The last ruler of an independent Egypt was Cleopatra. After her defeat, Egypt became a Roman province. The treasures of the Pharaohs were stolen and much of Egypt's grain was taken to Rome.

# Index